S0-DVC-268

COLONISTS

David Haugen, Book Editor

San Diego • Detroit • New York • San Francisco • Cleveland • New Haven, Conn. • Waterville, Maine • London • Munich

For more information, contact
The Gale Group, Inc.
27500 Drake Rd.
Farmington Hills, MI 48331-3535
Or you can visit our Internet site at http://www.gale.com

Photo credits: Cover © Francis G. Mayer / CORBIS; page 5, 7, 15, 26, 29 © North Wind Picture Archives; page 6, 8 (top) © Blackbirch Archives; page 8 (middle) © Corel; page 8 (bottom), 9 (all), 11, 13, 23 © Library of Congress; page 17 © The Pierpont Morgan Library / Art Resorce, NY; page 21 © National Portrait Gallery, Smithsonian Institution / Art Resource, NY;

LIBRARY OF CONGRESS CATALOGING-IN-PUBLICATION DATA

Colonists / by David Haugen
p. cm. — (Voices from the American Revolution)
Summary: A history of the Revolutionary War, as told through diary excerpts, letters, and personal narratives from colonists and other eyewitnesses.
Includes index.
ISBN 1-4103-0448-5 (lib. bdg. : alk. paper)

Printed in the United States
10 9 8 7 6 5 4 3 2 1

Contents

Living Through Revolutionary Times

Although the Revolutionary War (1775–1783) was fought primarily between colonial Americans and the British, the conflict was in many ways a civil war. When the first shots were fired at the Battle of Lexington, not all Americans were in favor of war with Britain. It is estimated that for every patriot who embraced independence from English rule, there were a like number of colonists who remained loyal to Britain. Furthermore, a third of the colonial population desired to simply stay neutral in the conflict. Far from uniting the colonists against Britain, then, the Revolution divided many communities and often turned neighbors against one another when questions of loyalty arose.

While many colonists—whether rebel or loyalist (those who sided with Britain)—took up arms in the great struggle, a larger percent of the population did not participate directly in the fighting. Some men and women remained on the home front to run their farms or businesses. Maintaining a family's livelihood was an important concern during the war since many farmers and tradesmen did volunteer to go off to fight. Those family members left behind had to keep their farms and shops running. In the South, most African American slaves were kept out of the fighting both to continue laboring on the large plantations and to keep them from escaping to freedom.

The fact that they did not shoulder a weapon did not mean that the colonists on the home front stayed out of the war. Those men and women with rebel or loyalist sympathies aided their sides in many ways. Some mended uniforms, provided food, or manufactured weapons and ammunition to help supply the armies. Others opened their homes to wounded soldiers. Still others acted as spies and guided soldiers through unfamiliar territory or passed along vital information about enemy troop

While many colonists took up arms in the fight for America's independence, others stayed behind and forged weapons (pictured), acted as spies, and provided soldiers with food and shelter.

movements. Those who were brave enough spoke publicly about their loyalties. Such individuals, however, were subject to their neighbors' abuse—and possibly a tarring and feathering—if their opinions were not shared by the majority of their community.

The war also forcibly intruded upon the lives of the colonists. Those who lived within the paths of the marching armies were preyed upon by both the Continentals and the British. Hungry soldiers might steal a farmer's livestock; supply officers might commandeer (or take by military authority) a tradesman's wagons and carts. Typically a colonist was not reimbursed for his losses. Occasionally, a kind Continental officer might pay for the items in newly printed paper money. The payment, however, was always a token gesture since the money printed by the Continental Congress became more and more worthless as the war dragged on. In fact, the Congress had to authorize the printing of so much paper money to pay its war debts that it sparked high inflation as early as 1776. Common necessities, such as sugar, became so unaffordable in shops that many colonists had to turn to the growing black market to obtain these items.

Paper money issued by the Continental Congress lost value as the war continued.

Other hardships also plagued those colonists caught on or near a battlefield. Besides suffering looting, farmers might have their land trampled or ruined by the opposing armies. Homesteads near battle sites were often set ablaze or otherwise destroyed by cannon fire. When Boston was under siege by patriot forces in 1775 and 1776, some outlying parts of the town were destroyed in this manner. Other homes in the town were torn down by the British who had run low on wood fuel. Civilians caught within Boston—whether patriot or loyalist—also faced severe food shortages and various epidemics during the eleven-month siege. Throughout the war, the British also burned several colonial towns in retribution for aid given to the rebel army. Such actions, however, often steeled the nerve of the patriots within the town and even swayed some neutral colonists to take up the cause of independence.

Although several colonial communities suffered the ravages of war, many civilians—especially those on the western frontier and in the Deep South—were left unscathed by the Revolution. Frontiersmen who did not join the patriot or loyalist cause remained as self-sufficient as before the war. They had more to fear from hostile Indians than from the Continental or British armies. News of the war, passed by word of mouth, was sometimes the only contact the more secluded colonists had with the progress of the fighting.

This engraving depicts British soldiers as they plunder a colonist's home. Both British and Continental soldiers stole from colonists during the course of the war.

Whether caught in harm's way or left relatively untouched by the years of bloodshed, colonists during the Revolution had a stake in the events that swirled around them. The Declaration of Independence and the principles it embodies would help form the blueprint for a new nation that would arise after seven years of fighting. Patriots and loyalists who remained in America were then faced with shaping the character of this collection of independent states. They were also challenged with creating a constitution to define the union of these states. Both would prove to be daunting tasks but ones that were within reach of those men and women who had been tempered by the fires of revolution.

CHRONOLOGY OF THE REVOLUTION

MARCH 1765

King George III of England approves the Stamp Act, which taxes the American colonies to help pay for the French and Indian War. Colonists protest the tax as unfair because it was levied without colonial representation in Parliament.

AUGUST 1768

Boston firebrand Samuel Adams calls for a boycott of English imports. In response, England sends troops to the colonies to maintain order.

MARCH 1770

Five colonists are killed after a brief confrontation with British soldiers outside Boston's Customs House. Known as the Boston Massacre, the event adds to the tensions in the colonies.

SEPTEMBER 1774

The colonies send delegates to the First Continental Congress to address the tensions between England and America.

JULY 1776

IN CONGRESS, JULY 4, 1776.
A DECLARATION
BY THE REPRESENTATIVES OF THE
UNITED STATES OF AMERICA,
IN GENERAL CONGRESS ASSEMBLED.

The Continental Congress votes to declare American independence. It adopts Thomas Jefferson's Declaration of Independence as its testimonial of British abuses and American resolve to be free.

DECEMBER 1776

Washington stages a daring surprise attack on Trenton, New Jersey, where Hessian mercenaries working for the British have camped for the winter.

OCTOBER 1777

While Washington fights battles in Pennsylvania, General Horatio Gates achieves a resounding victory over British general John Burgoyne's army near Saratoga, New York. Burgoyne's army is the first British command to surrender to patriot forces.

King George III of England

APRIL–AUGUST 1775

• The British commander in Boston sends units to nearby Lexington and Concord to seize colonial weapons and ammunition. The colonists are alerted to his move, and militia units from neighboring colonies converge on Concord to stop the British advance. The two sides exchange fire, and the British are forced to retreat back to Boston.

• The Continental Congress meets again to discuss breaking free from English rule. It appoints George Washington as the commander of military forces in America.

• Before Washington can arrive to take charge of the patriot units around Boston, the British advance and achieve a costly victory at the Battle of Bunker Hill.

• In August, after finally hearing of the skirmish at Lexington and Concord, King George III declares the colonies to be in revolt.

FEBRUARY 1778–JUNE 1779

• Benjamin Franklin helps broker a formal military alliance between France and America.

• France declares war on England.

• Spain officially declares war on England.

JULY–OCTOBER 1781

French troops arrive in Rhode Island. Their commander, the Comte de Rochambeau, persuades Washington to stage an offensive in the South against British forces under Lord Charles Cornwallis. With the French fleet cutting off Cornwallis's retreat by sea, the combined American and French armies surround the British army at Yorktown, Virginia, and force Cornwallis to surrender on October 19.

SEPTEMBER 1783

The Treaty of Paris is signed and the war ends, despite the fact that the Continental Congress would not finish ratifying the treaty until the following year. In November, George Washington resigns his commission as head of the Continental army.

George Washington

John Tudor

Eyewitness to the Boston Massacre

On March 5, 1770, outside the Custom House where taxes for Boston Harbor were collected, a young colonist taunted a British soldier on sentry duty. The soldier reacted by clubbing the disrespectful colonist with the butt of his gun. Onlookers soon came to the colonist's defense, and an angry mob formed. They insulted the sentry and threw snowballs at him.

British captain Thomas Preston got word of the incident and assembled six soldiers and a corporal to reestablish order at the Custom House. Arriving on the scene, Preston held the crowd at bay while the mood grew darker. Eventually one of the soldiers was knocked down. Getting to his feet, he fired into the crowd because he thought Preston had given the order. Other soldiers followed suit, and the mob scattered. Three colonists were dead in the street and another seven were wounded. Two of those wounded died later.

Fearing that the continued presence of the soldiers would provoke rebellion after the massacre, concerned citizens petitioned the lieutenant governor to have the troops moved out of the town. After some hesitancy, the lieutenant governor recognized the danger and recommended to the military commander in Boston that the troops be sent to nearby Castle William, a fort on the edge of town. The colonists were overjoyed, believing they had won a small victory against British tyranny. John Tudor witnessed the whole affair and wrote the following account of it.

Glossary

- **multitudes:** crowds
- **regiment:** unit of soldiers

This unhappy affair began by some boys and young fellows throwing snow balls at the sentry placed at the Customhouse door. On which 8 or 9 soldiers came to his assistance. Soon after a number of people collected, when the Captain commanded the soldiers to fire, which they did and 3 men were killed on the spot and several mortally wounded, one of whom died the next morning. The Captain soon drew off his soldiers up to the main guard, or the consequences might have been terrible, for on the guns firing the people were alarmed and set the bells a-ringing as if for fire, which drew multitudes to the place of action. Lieutenant Governor [Thomas] Hutchinson, who was commander-in-chief,

British soldiers shot and killed three colonists and wounded seven others in what became known as the Boston Massacre.

was sent for and came to the council chamber, where some of the magistrates attended. The Governor desired the multitude about 10 o'clock to separate and go home peaceably and he would do all in his power that justice should be done, etc. . . . But the people insisted that the soldiers should be ordered to their barracks first before they would separate, which being done the people separated about one o'clock. . . . Tuesday A.M. the inhabitants met at Faneuil Hall and after some pertinent speeches, chose a committee of 15 gentlemen to wait on the Lieutenant Governor in council to request the immediate removal of the troops. The message was in these words: That it is the unanimous opinion of this meeting, that the inhabitants and soldiery can no longer live together in safety; that nothing can rationally be expected to restore the peace of the town and prevent blood and carnage but the removal of the troops. . . . His honor's reply was, "Gentlemen I am extremely sorry for the unhappy difference and especially of the last evening," and signifying that it was not in his power to remove the troops.

The above reply was not satisfactory to the inhabitants. . . . In the afternoon the town adjourned to Dr. Sewill's meetinghouse . . . when they chose a committee to wait on the Lieutenant Governor to let him and the council know that nothing less will satisfy the people, than a total and immediate removal of the troops out of the town. His honor laid before the council the vote of the town. The council thereon expressed themselves to be unanimously of opinion that it was absolutely necessary for his Majesty's service, the good order of the town, that the troops should be immediately removed out of the town. His honor communicated this advice of the council to Colonel Dalrymple and desired he would order the troops down to Castle William. After the Colonel had seen the vote of the council he gave his word and honor to the town's committee that both the regiments should be removed without delay. The committee returned to the town meeting and Mr. [John] Hancock, chairman of the committee, read their report as above, which was received with a shout and clap of hands, which made the meetinghouse ring.

John Tudor, personal account of the Boston Massacre, 1770.

GEORGE HEWES

Joining the Tea Party

In 1773, the East India Company—England's largest importer of tea—was facing bankruptcy and applied to Parliament for a special license to sell tea directly to the colonies. They hoped to avoid the taxes usually levied in England. The English prime minister agreed. Word of this deal angered most colonial tea merchants because the East India Company only traded with a few loyalist merchants in the colonies; the majority of merchants had to deal with other companies who were not receiving the special exemption from England's taxes. Thus, those who were favored by the East India Company could undersell the other merchants. On November 28, the Dartmouth, *the first of the East India ships, reached Boston Harbor. Representatives of the angry colonists confronted the captain, Francis Rotch, and demanded that he to return to England without unloading his wares. Rotch complained that if he did not deliver his tea, he would be ruined financially. The Bostonians gave him twenty days to comply. On December 16, the eve of the deadline, Boston politician Samuel Adams convened a meeting attended by seven thousand colonists. Fed up with the delays, the crowd called for action. The meeting adjourned, and when night came, a gang of colonists—many dressed as Indians or otherwise disguised—boarded the* Dartmouth *and two other East India ships that had arrived in port. With hatchets and crowbars, the mob broke open 342 tea chests, and dumped ninety thousand pounds of East India tea into Boston Harbor. In the following memoir, one participant, Georges Hewes, recalls the events of the evening.*

It was now evening, and I immediately dressed myself in the costume of an Indian, equipped with a small hatchet, which I and my associates denominated the tomahawk, with which, and a club, after having painted my face and hands with coal dust in the shop of a blacksmith, I repaired to Griffin's wharf, where the ships lay that contained the tea. When I first appeared in the street after being thus disguised, I fell in with many who were dressed, equipped and painted as I was, and who fell in with me and marched in order to the place of our destination.

When we arrived at the wharf, there were three of our number who assumed an authority to direct our operations, to which we readily submitted. They divided us into three parties, for the purpose of boarding the three ships which contained the tea at the same time. The name of him who commanded the division to which I was assigned was Leonard Pitt. The names of the other commanders I never knew. We were immediately

Disguised as Indians, colonists dumped ninety thousand pounds of tea into Boston Harbor to protest England's tax on tea.

ordered by the respective commanders to board all the ships at the same time, which we promptly obeyed. The commander of the division to which I belonged, as soon as we were on board the ship, appointed me boatswain, and ordered me to go to the captain and demand of him the keys to the hatches and a dozen candles. I made the demand accordingly, and the captain promptly replied, and delivered the articles; but requested me at the same time to do no damage to the ship or rigging. We then were ordered by our commander to open the hatches and take out all the chests of tea and throw them overboard, and we immediately proceeded to execute his orders, first cutting and splitting the chests with our tomahawks, so as thoroughly to expose them to the effects of the water.

In about three hours from the time we went on board, we had thus broken and thrown overboard every tea chest to be found in the ship, while those in the other ships were disposing of the tea in the same way, at the same time. We were surrounded by British armed ships, but no attempt was made to resist us.

We then quietly retired to our several places of residence, without having any conversation with each other, or taking any measures to discover who were our associates; nor do I recollect of our having had the knowledge of the name of a single individual concerned in that affair, except that of Leonard Pitt, the commander of my division, whom I have mentioned. There appeared to be an understanding that each individual should volunteer his services, keep his own secret, and risk the consequence for himself. No disorder took place during that transaction, and it was observed at that time that the stillest night ensued that Boston had enjoyed for many months.

James Hawkes, *A Retrospect of the Boston Tea Party with a Memoir of George R.T. Hewes, Survivor of the Little Band of Patriots Who Drowned the Tea in Boston Harbour in 1773*. New York: S. S. Bliss, 1834.

Glossary

- **denominated:** referred to as
- **repaired to:** went to
- **rigging:** ropes, tackles, and sails

Ann Hulton

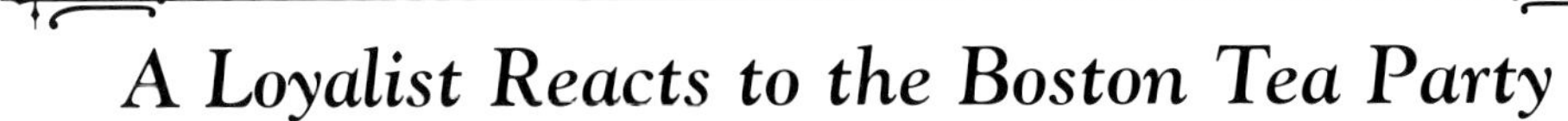

A Loyalist Reacts to the Boston Tea Party

Ann Hulton was the sister of Henry Hulton, the customs commissioner for Boston between 1767 and 1776. In a letter to the wife of Adam Lightbody, a merchant in England, Hulton describes the effects of the tea party upon those Boston citizens who were still loyal to King George III. Hulton was a loyalist herself, and she had witnessed the continual insults hurled at her brother and other customs officials as they tried to carry out their jobs. She feared for the lives of the officials as they were forced to seek refuge in Castle William (where British troops were garrisoned) and obliged to stay there for weeks after the events of December 16, 1773.

I suppose you will have heard long before this arrives of the fate of the Tea. Whilst this was in suspence, the commissioners of the Customs and the Tea Consignees were obliged to seek refuge at the Castle. My Brother happened to be there on a visit of a long engagement to Col. Lesley when those other Gentlemen came over. He continued there about twenty days, in the mean time visiting his own House (about 8 Miles from the Castle) several times. . . . After the destruction of the Tea, my Brother returned Home and the other Commissioners Left the Castle. The violent fury of the People having subsided a little. One would have thought before that all the Malice that Earth and Hell could raise were pointed against the Governor [Thomas Hutchinson]. Mr. Paxton (one of the commissioners) and the Tea Consignees, two of whom are the Governors Sons, the others are Mr. Clark a respecta[ble] Old Gentleman and his Sons, with two other Merchants Mr. Haliwell another Commissioner and likewise of this Country was an object of their threats.

The Tea Consignees remain Still at the Castle. Six weeks since the Tea was destroyed, and there is no prospect of their ever returning and residing in Boston with Safety. This place, and all the Towns about entered into a written agreement not to afford them any Shelter or protection, so that they are not only banished from

Glossary

- **in suspence:** pending
- **consignees:** custodians of merchandise
- **malice:** hatred
- **prospect:** hope
- **interest:** livelihood and social standing

After the Boston Tea Party, people who remained loyal to King George III were often insulted, ridiculed, and sometimes even forced out of town.

their families and homes, but their retreat is cut off, and their interest greatly injured by ruining their Trade.

It is indeed a severe case, and can hardly be credited, I think, that the Governors Sons should be treated as fugitives and outlaws in their own Country. One of them lately went from the Castle, and with his Wife to her Fathers House, a Gentleman at Plymouth 40 Miles from Boston. They had no sooner arrived there, but the Bells tolled and the Town Assembling instantly went to the House, demanded that Mr. Hutchinson should depart immediately out of the Town. Colonel Watson his father in law, spoke to them, saying that it was so late at Night, and the Weather so severe, that Mr. H. and his wife could not without great inconvenience remove from his house that night, but promised them, they should go in the Morning by 9 o'Clock. The time came, and they were not gone, when the Town bells tolled again, and the people gathered about the house. Upon which the Young Couple set off in a great snow storm. And nobody knows since where they are.

Ann Hulton, letter to Mrs. Adam Lightbody.

ALEXANDER GRAYDON

Persecuting Loyalists

During the Revolution, many colonists refused to support the rebellion. Though some tried to remain neutral, others thought of themselves as British subjects and were therefore loyal to the king of England. Townspeople and villagers were commonly divided in their reaction to the call for American independence. In communities where the rebel spirit ran high, colonial loyalists were often harassed by their prorevolutionary neighbors. Sometimes gangs of rebellion-minded citizens would hound the loyalists and attempt to run them out of town. This persecution might begin with insults and snubbing, but it could escalate to physical abuse and public humiliation. A popular form of punishment was to cover the loyalist in hot tar and feathers and drag him through the streets in a cart.

In the following selection from his memoirs, Alexander Graydon of Pennsylvania describes one instance in 1775 in which a loyalist named Dr. Kearsley was tormented by a band of rebel sympathizers in Philadelphia.

Among the disaffected in Philadelphia, Doctor Kearsley was pre-eminently ardent and rash. An extremely zealous Loyalist, and impetuous in his temper, he had given much umbrage to the whigs; and if I am not mistaken, he had been detected in some hostile machinations. Hence he was deemed a proper subject for the fashionable punishment of tarring, feathering and carting. He was seized at his own door by a party of the militia, and, in the attempt to resist them, received a wound in his hand from a bayonet. Being overpowered, he was placed in a cart provided for the purpose, and amidst a multitude of boys and idlers, paraded through the streets to the tune of the rogue's march. I happened to be at the coffee-house when the concourse arrived there. They made a halt, while the Doctor, foaming with rage and indignation, without his hat, his wig dishevelled and bloody from his wounded hand, stood up in the cart and called for a bowl of punch. It was quickly handed to him; when so vehement was his thirst that he drained it of its contents before he took it from his lips.

What were the feelings of others on this lawless proceeding, I know not, but mine, I must confess, revolted at the spectacle. I was shocked at seeing a lately respected citizen so cruelly vilified, and was imprudent enough to say that, had I been a magistrate, I would, at every hazard, have interposed my authority in suppression of the

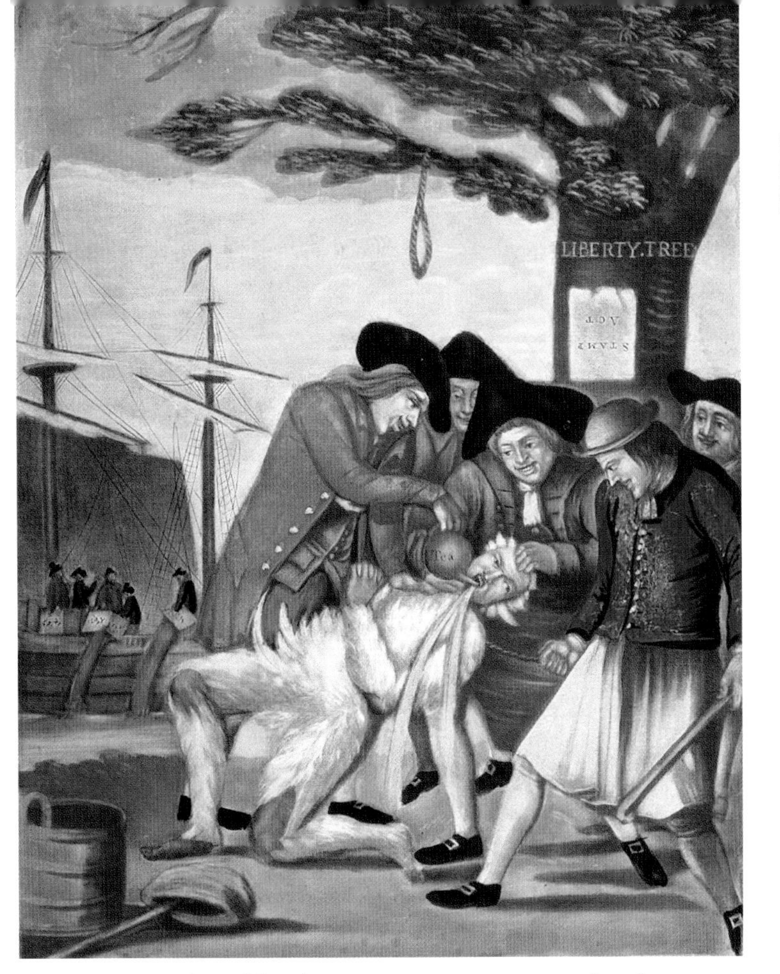

Colonial loyalists were sometimes tarred and feathered, then dragged through town in a cart.

Glossary

- **disaffected:** rebellious
- **pre-eminently:** exceedingly
- **ardent:** passionate
- **zealous:** enthusiastic
- **impetuous:** hasty
- **umbrage:** offense
- **whigs:** rebel political party
- **machinations:** schemes
- **militia:** local soldiers
- **bayonet:** long blade
- **concourse:** parade
- **vehement:** intense
- **vilified:** humiliated
- **wanted:** lacked
- **lenity:** gentleness

outrage. But this was not the only instance which convinced me that I wanted nerves for a revolutionist. It must be admitted, however, that the conduct of the populace was marked by a lenity which peculiarly distinguished the cradle of our republicanism. Tar and feathers had been dispensed with, and excepting the injury he had received in his hand, no sort of violence was offered by the mob to their victim. But to a man of high spirit, as the Doctor was, the indignity in its lightest form was sufficient to madden him: it probably had this effect, since his conduct became so extremely outrageous that it was thought necessary to confine him. From the city he was soon after removed to Carlisle, where he died during the war.

Alexander Graydon, *Memoirs of His Own Time, with Reminiscences of the Men and Events of the Revolution.* Ed. John Stockton Littrell. Philadelphia: Lindsay & Blakiston, 1846.

JOHN ANDREWS

Living Through the Siege of Boston

In June 1775, the British, who had just won a victory at the Battle of Bunker Hill, retreated into Boston. Colonial forces encircled the town and quickly laid siege to it. Although the British soldiers were the target of the siege, the citizens of Boston suffered as well. Food and fuel shortages were common. Many people chose to leave the town. The people who stayed behind did so for various reasons. John Andrews was a Bostonian who endured the siege to protect his property from destruction and theft. In the following letter to a friend, William Barrell, Andrews writes of the inconveniences of living under the siege.

Its hard to stay cooped up here and feed upon salt provissions . . . I find an absolute necessity to be here myself, as the soldiery think they have a license to plunder every one's house and store who leaves the town. . . .

We have now and then a carcase offered for sale in the market, which formerly we would not have picked up in the street; but bad as it is, it readily sells for eight pence lawful money per lb., and a quarter of lamb when it makes its appearance, which is rarely once a week, sells for a dollar, weighing only three or three and a half pounds. To such shifts has the necessity of the times drove us; wood not scarcely to be got at twenty two shillings a cord. Was it not for a triffle of salt provisions that we have, 'twould be impossible for us to live. Pork and beans one day, and beans and pork another, and fish when we can catch it. Am necessitated to submit to such living or risque the little all I have in the world, which consists in my stock of goods and furniture to the amount of between two and three thousand sterling, as it's said without scruple that those who leave the town forfeit all the effects they leave behind.

Glossary

- **provissions:** provisions, food
- **carcase:** carcass, animal body
- **cord:** an eight-foot-long, four-foot-wide bundle
- **risque:** risk
- **scruple:** qualm

John Andrews, "Letters of John Andrews, Esq., of Boston, 1772–1776" in Winthrop Sargent, ed., *Massachusetts Historical Society Proceedings.* Vol. 8, 1866.

Peter Van Schaak

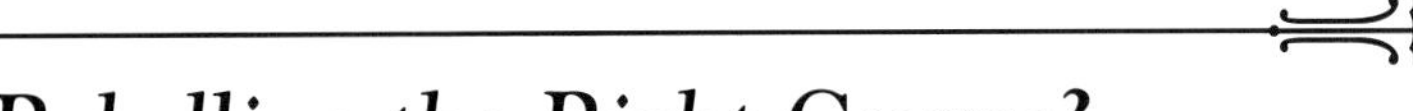

Is Rebellion the Right Course?

Roughly one out of every three colonists remained neutral during the war because they were not convinced that armed revolution was the answer to the problems between England and America. Peter Van Schaak was a colonist from New York who, like all Americans, had to question his loyalties when war broke out. In the following journal entry from January 1776, Van Schaak argues his own preference for a middle ground between slavish dependence on Britain and the chaos that he fears independence will bring.

There are perhaps few questions relating to government of more difficulty than that at present subsisting between Great Britain and the Colonies. It originated about the degree of subordination we owe to the British Parliament, but by a rapid progress it seems now to be whether we are members of the empire or not. . . .

If it be asked how we come to be subject to the authority of the British Parliament, I answer, by the same compact which entitles us to the benefits of the British constitution and its laws; and that we derive advantage even from some kind of subordination, whatever the degree of it should be, is evident, because, without such a controlling common umpire, the colonies must become independent states, which would be introductive of anarchy and confusion among ourselves.

Some kind of dependence being then, in my idea, necessary for our own happiness, I would choose to see a claim made of a constitution which shall concede this point, as, before that is done by us and rejected by the mother country, I cannot see any principle of regard for my country which will authorize me in taking up arms, as absolute dependence and independence are two extremes which I would avoid; for, should we succeed in the latter, we shall still be in a sea of uncertainty and have to fight among ourselves for that constitution we aim at.

Henry Cruger Van Schaak, *Life of Peter Van Schaak.* New York: Appleton, 1842.

Glossary

- **subordination:** servitude
- **compact:** agreement, contract
- **be introductive of anarchy:** bring forth lawlessness
- **the mother country:** England

JOHN WITHERSPOON

God Favors the Humble Patriots

Clergyman John Witherspoon became the president of the College of New Jersey (which was later renamed Princeton University) in 1768. In the following sermon given on May 17, 1776, Witherspoon assures his congregation that God is involved in the now year-old contest between Britain and the American colonies. He asserts that the recent successes the colonists have enjoyed in their fight for freedom—including the British evacuation of Boston—reveal that God has not forsaken those who have suffered at the hands of tyrants and oppressors. Witherspoon, however, is quick to remind his audience that Americans must accept this divine intervention with humility, for boasting of success is a sure way to lose God's favor.

Glossary

- **interposition:** intervention
- **hitherto:** previously
- **designs:** plans
- **dissembled:** falsely reported
- **moment:** importance
- **an arm of flesh:** human deeds
- **ostentatious:** pretentious
- **vaunting:** prideful
- **abase:** lower
- **exulting:** gloating

From what has been said upon this subject, you may see what ground there is to give praise to God for his favours already bestowed on us, respecting the public cause. It would be a criminal inattention not to observe the singular interposition of providence hitherto, in behalf of the American colonies. It is however impossible for me in a single discourse, as well as improper at this time, to go thro' every step of our past transactions. I must therefore content myself with a few remarks. How many discoveries have been made of the designs of enemies in Britain and among ourselves, in a manner as unexpected to us as to them, and in such season as to prevent their effect? What surprising success has attended our encounters in almost every instance? Has not the boasted discipline of regular and veteran soldiers been turned into confusion and dismay before the new and maiden courage of freemen in defence of their property and right? In what great mercy has blood been spared on the side of this injured country? Some important victories in the south have been gained with so little loss, that enemies will probably think it has been dissembled; as many, even of ourselves thought, till time rendered it undeniable. But these were comparatively of small moment. The signal advantage we have gained by the evacuation of Boston, and the shameful flight of the army and navy of Britain, was brought about without the loss of a man. To all this we may add, that the counsels of our enemies have been visibly confounded, so that I believe I may say with truth, that there is hardly any step which they have taken, but it has operated strongly against themselves, and been more in our favour than if they had followed a contrary course.

John Witherspoon assured his patriot congregation that God was on their side in their fight for independence.

While we give praise to God the supreme disposer of all events, for his interposition in our behalf, let us guard against the dangerous error of trusting in, or boasting of an arm of flesh. It has given me great uneasiness to read some ostentatious, vaunting expressions in our news papers, though happily I think, much restrained of late. Let us not return to them again. If I am not mistaken, not only the holy scriptures in general, and the truths of the glorious gospel in particular, but the whole course of providence seems intended to abase the pride of man, and lay the vainglorious in the dust. How many instances does history furnish us with of those who after exulting over, and despising their enemies, were signally and shamefully defeated. The truth is, I believe, the remark may be applied universally, and we may say, that thro' the whole frame of nature, and the whole system of human life, that which promises most, performs the least. The flowers of finest colour seldom have the sweetest fragrance. The trees of quickest growth or fairest form, are seldom of the greatest value or duration. Deep waters move with least noise. Men who think most are seldom talkative. And I think it holds as much in war as in any thing, that every boaster is a coward.

John Witherspoon, "The Dominion of Providence over the Passions of Men," May 17, 1776.

HENRY LAURENS

The Problem of Slavery

When the Declaration of Independence was issued in 1776, colonial patriots proclaimed that they were fighting for liberty and equality. Those admirable principles, however, did not extend to the many thousands of black men and women who had been brought to America as slaves. The contradiction was glaring to most Americans, and it remained a source of controversy throughout the war. Colonists, especially in the northern colonies, argued that slavery was morally wrong and out of step with the new national creed that professed that "all men are created equal." Furthermore, many freed blacks and slaves were serving in the ranks of the Continental army and fighting alongside their white brethren for a freedom they hoped to share. It would be difficult to acknowledge their contribution and yet deny them the rewards of victory. The southern colonies, however, were coming to rely on slave labor to run their agricultural economies. Although some southern colonies agreed to end the importation of slaves, they were not willing to grant freedom or civil rights to the slaves already in America. The English, who had long since abandoned slavery, seized upon the inconsistency in colonial ideals. They tried to entice slaves away from the colonial cause with offers of freedom and fair treatment. A number of blacks did cast their lot with the British during the war in anticipation of liberation and the protection of English rights. Many of those did not find the British to be any more liberal than the slaves' colonial masters. In the following August 1776 letter, Henry Laurens, a member of the South Carolina provincial congress, discusses his own distaste for slavery despite being a slaveholder. He also points out the hypocrisy of the British attempts to lure slaves away from the colonists.

My Negroes, all to a man, are strongly attached to me; hitherto not one of them has attempted to desert; on the contrary, those who are more exposed hold themselves always ready to fly from the enemy in case of a sudden descent. Many hundreds of that colour have been stolen and decoyed by the servants of King George the Third. Captains of British ships of war and noble lords have busied themselves in such inglorious pilferage, to the disgrace of their master and disgrace of their cause. These Negroes were first enslaved by the English. . . . Men of war, forts, castles, governors, companies and committees are employed and authorized by the English parliament to protect, regulate and extend the slave trade. Negroes are brought by

Englishmen and sold as slaves to Americans. Bristol, Liverpool, Manchester, Birmingham, etc., etc., live upon the slave trade. The British parliament now employ their men-of-war to steal those Negroes from the Americans to whom they had sold them, pretending to set the poor wretches free, but basely trepan and sell them into tenfold worse slavery in the West Indies, where probably they will become the property of Englishmen again, and of some who sit in parliament. What meanness! What complicated wickedness appears in this scene! O England, how changed! How fallen! . . . I abhor slavery. I was born in a country where slavery had been established by British kings and parliaments, as well as by the laws of that country ages before my existence. I found the Christian religion and slavery growing under the same authority and cultivation. I nevertheless disliked it. In former days there was no combating the prejudices of men supported by interest; the day I hope is approaching when, from principles of gratitude as well as justice, every man will strive to be foremost in showing his readiness to comply with the golden rule.

Henry Laurens, letter to John Laurens, August 1776.

Glossary

- **hitherto:** thus far
- **more exposed:** with more opportunity for escape
- **pilferage:** robbery
- **men of war:** fighting ships
- **trepan:** entrap
- **abhor:** hate

Henry Laurens recognized the contradiction in owning slaves and fighting for liberty and equality.

ABIGAIL ADAMS

Dealing with Profiteers

One of the main concerns of Americans during the war was that devious merchants might take advantage of the patriots' needs and inflate prices to make quick profits. Local governments and civic action committees tried to regulate selling prices and root out any merchant who seemed to be monopolizing common military or civilian necessities. In a letter written to her husband in July 1777, Abigail Adams, the future first lady of the United States, describes one instance in which the women of Boston confronted a warehouse owner suspected of hoarding coffee.

You must know that there is a great scarcity of sugar and coffee, articles which the female part of the state is very loath to give up, especially whilst they consider the scarcity occasioned by the merchants having secreted a large quantity. There had been much rout and noise in the town for several weeks. Some stores had been opened by a number of people, and the coffee and sugar carried into the market and dealt out by pounds. It was rumored that an eminent, wealthy, stingy merchant (who is a bachelor) had a hogshead of coffee in his store, which he refused to sell to the committee under six shillings per pound.

A number of females, some say a hundred, some say more, assembled with a cart and trucks, marched down to the warehouse and demanded the keys, which he refused to deliver. Upon which, one of them seized him by his neck and tossed him into the cart. Upon his finding no quarter, he delivered the keys, when they tipped up the cart and discharged him; then opened the warehouse, hoisted out the coffee themselves, put it into the truck and drove off.

It was reported that he had personal chastisement among them; but this, I believe, was not true. A large concourse of men stood amazed, silent spectators of the whole transaction.

Glossary

- **secreted:** hidden
- **hogshead:** large cask
- **quarter:** mercy
- **had personal chastisement:** had been physically punished
- **concourse:** gathering

Charles Francis Adams, ed., *Letters to Mrs. Adams, the Wife of John Adams*. 3rd ed. Boston: C.C. Little and J. Brown, 1841.

JOSEPH EGGLESTON JR.

Worthless Paper Money

Without enough financial reserves to pay for equipping the Continental army or to pay its soldiers, the Continental Congress was forced—as early as 1775—to print paper currency to cover its expenses. As the war dragged on, the amount of required cash grew, so Congress printed more and more money. Almost immediately, the value of the paper currency declined, and it continued to decline as more of it was put into circulation.

In the following letter from September 1777, Joseph Eggleston Jr., a soldier in the colonial army, writes to his father, that, because of the continued devaluation of colonial money, prices of all necessities have run high. He then jokes that, in light of recent American victories, the rampant inflation is a greater threat to the colonies than the British.

The prices of every kind of article here would astonish you. You desire I would procure you a good beaver hatt and some other articles. In answer to which part of your letter I would inform you that goods are 200 per cent dearer than they were in Virginia when I left it. I was obliged to buy a hat a few days past, and paid 18 dollars for one of an inferior kind. Boots sell for the moderate price of 21 dollars; broad cloth £12 a yard. Rum is 20/the quart; whiskey 10/. Every other article bears a proportionate price.

But I turn from this prospect to one that can be contemplated with much greater pleasure. I mean our military affairs; for it is my fixed opinion that America has much more to fear from the effects of the large quantities of paper money than from the operations of Howe and all the British generals. [British general John] Burgoyne has been defeated by [American] General [Benedict] Arnold, has lost his tents, baggage, etc., and is retreating with his broken forces towards Ticonderoga. . . . I will just inform you that the whole army, from General Washington downwards, are in high spirits.

Joseph Eggleston Jr., letter to Joseph Eggleston Sr., September 2, 1777. The J. Pierpont Morgan Library.

- **dearer:** more expensive

JACOB DUCHÉ

A Plea to End the Rebellion

While imprisoned by the British, Jacob Duché pleaded with General George Washington to end the bloodshed of the war by negotiating peace.

In the early days of the Revolution, the Reverend Jacob Duché was an outspoken patriot. He even served as the chaplain to the Continental Congress at Philadelphia. When that city was captured by British general William Howe in 1777, Duché was put in jail for his treasonous sympathies. There, Duché seemed to have a change of heart, and in October of that year, he wrote to General George Washington. In his letter, excerpted below, Duché begged the patriot leader to renounce the rebellion and lead the colonies back into the British fold. Washington ignored the advice. Duché eventually sailed to England. He did not return to his homeland until 1792.

Perhaps it may be said that "it is better to die than to be slaves." This, indeed, is a splendid maxim in theory; and, perhaps, in some instances, may be found experimentally true. But where there is the least probability of any happy accommodation, surely wisdom and humanity call for some sacrifices to be made to prevent inevitable destruction. You will know that there is but one invincible bar to such an accommodation; could this be removed, other obstacles might readily be overcome.

'Tis to you, and you alone, your bleeding country looks, and calls aloud for this sacrifice. Your arm alone has strength sufficient to remove this bar. May Heaven inspire you with the glorious resolution of exerting this strength at so interesting a crisis, and thus immortalizing yourself as a friend and guardian of your country.

Your penetrating eye needs not more explicit language to discern my meaning. With that prudence and delicacy, therefore, of which I know you to be possessed, represent to Congress the indispensable necessity of rescinding the hasty and ill-advised Declaration of Independency. Recommend . . . an immediate cessation of hostilities. Let the controversy be taken up where that Declaration left it. . . . Let men of clear and impartial characters, in or out of Congress, liberal in their sentiments, heretofore independent in their fortunes. . . . be appointed to confer with His Majesty's Commissioners. Let them, if they please, prepare some well-digested constitutional plan, to lay before them as the commencement of a negotiation. When they have gone thus far, I am confident that the most happy consequences will ensue. Unanimity will immediately take place through the different Provinces. Thousands who are now ardently wishing and praying for such a measure will step forth and declare themselves the zealous advocates of constitutional liberty, and millions will bless the Hero that left the field of war to decide this most important contest with the weapons of wisdom and humanity. . . .

Glossary

- **maxim:** adage, proverb
- **one invincible bar:** one obstacle (that is, the rebellion)
- **discern:** recognize
- **rescinding:** withdrawing
- **cessation:** end
- **liberal:** open-minded
- **well-digested:** well thought out
- **unanimity:** agreement, harmony
- **ardently:** passionately
- **zealous:** enthusiastic
- **advocates:** supporters

Jared Sparks, ed., *Correspondence of the American Revolution; Being Letters of Eminent Men to George Washington, from the Time of His Taking Command of the Army to the End of His Presidency.* Vol. 1. Boston: Little Brown, 1853.

FREDERIKA VON RIEDESEL

Prisoners in Boston

When British general John Burgoyne surrendered his army at the Battle of Saratoga in 1777, the German mercenaries in his command also became colonial prisoners. Baron von Riedesel, a major general, was one of the German who was captured. He and his wife joined many other prisoners of war as they were sent for detention in Boston. Frederika von Riedesel recorded the treatment she and her friends received in the city gripped by patriotic fervor. Eighteenth-century military codes stipulated that officers captured in battle were to be well treated, and in return they were bound by their honor not to flee from captivity. Typically, captured troops were not held for long, but were eventually returned to their homelands with the pledge that they could not return to fight in the war.

We finally reached Boston, and our troops were quartered in barracks not far away, on Winter Hill. We were put up at a farmer's house, where we were given only one room in the attic. My maids slept on the floor, and the men in the hall. Some straw on which I had spread our bedding was all we had for a long while on which to sleep, since I had nothing other than my field bed. Our host allowed us to eat downstairs in his room, where his whole family ate and slept together. The man was good, but his wife, in revenge for the bother we caused her, deliberately chose to vex us during our mealtime by combing her children's hair, which was full of vermin, often making us lose every bit of appetite, and when we asked her to do her combing outside, or at some other time, she replied, "It is my room; I see fit to stay and to comb my children now." We had to hold our silence, for otherwise she might have turned us out of the house. . . .

We stayed in this place three weeks before we were then taken to Cambridge, where we were put up in one of the most beautiful houses, previously the property of royalists. I have never seen a lovelier location. Seven families, partly relatives and partly friends, had leasehold estates here with gardens and magnificent houses and orchards nearby.

Glossary

- **quartered:** housed
- **vex:** annoy
- **royalists:** colonials loyal to England
- **reciprocate:** return

This woodcut depicts colonial general Philip Schuyler as he greets his prisoners of war, German baroness Frederika von Riedesel and her children.

All these estates were only about an eighth of a mile apart from one another. The owners gathered every afternoon at one of the homes or another, where they enjoyed themselves with music and dancing, living happily in comfort and harmony until, alas, the devastating war separated them all, leaving all the houses desolate with the exception of two, whose owners shortly thereafter were also obliged to flee.

None of our gentlemen were permitted to go to Boston. My curiosity and the desire to see [colonial] General [Philip] Schuyler's daughter, Mrs. Carter, impelled me to go, and I had dinner with her there several times. It is quite a pretty city, but inhabited by enthusiastic patriots and full of wicked people; the women, particularly, were horrid, casting ugly looks at me, and some of them even spitting when I passed by them. Mrs. Carter was gentle and good, like her parents, but her husband was a bad and treacherous person. They often visited us and ate with us and the other generals. We did our utmost to reciprocate their kindness. They seemed to feel very friendly toward us too, but it was during this time that this horrible Mr. Carter made the gruesome suggestion to the Americans, when the English General Howe had set fire to many villages and towns, to behead our generals, put the heads in small barrels, salt them, and send one of these barrels to the English for each village or town which they had set on fire. This beastly suggestion fortunately, however, was not adopted.

Frederika von Riedesel, letter concerning her imprisonment in Boston, 1777.

JAMES ALLEN

Robbed by the Military

James Allen, a Pennsylvania lawyer and landowner, was typical of many colonists who tried to remain neutral during the Revolution. In not taking sides, however, he often suffered the abuses of both the British and rebel armies. The following selection from his diary (dated October 15, 1777) tells of Continental militia ravaging the Pennsylvania farm country for useful items that could aid the war effort.

Gen Washington has issued orders to take the blankets, shoes, stockings, etc., of private families for the use of the army. This, together with the licentiousness, plundering, stealing and impressing of the military, will sink this country to perdition . . . .

The prevailing idea now is that no man has any property in what the publick has use for, and it is seldom they ask the owner; so wanton is this species of oppression called pressing that if they could by fair means get anything by a little trouble, they chuse to take private property by violence if somewhat nearer at hand. This I have seen in many instances, and felt in my own case. When the hospital and publick works were erected in this little town, I offered to supply them with wood at a reasonable rate, to avoid being plundered; yet they have hitherto gone on cutting my timber, burning my fences and taking bricks from me, rather than employ some of the many idle men they have in cutting wood . . . Yesterday a farmer sold me his whole brood of turkeys and fowls on receiving information that a neighbour, with whom he had a law suit 3 years ago, had informed the militia, who were setting out to take them away. It is probable they will soon plunder me of them, as every night they steal my poultry.

Glossary

- **licentiousness:** recklessness
- **impressing:** forcing citizens into military service
- **perdition:** hell
- **prevailing:** widespread
- **wanton:** merciless
- **pressing:** taking by right of military necessity
- **chuse:** choose
- **hitherto:** thus far

James Allen, "Diary," *Pennsylvania Magazine of History and Biography*, 9, 1885.

For More Information

Books

Ruth Dean, *Life in the American Colonies*. San Diego: Lucent, 1999.

Linda Grant Depauw, *Founding Mothers: Women of America in the Revolutionary Era*. New York: Houghton Mifflin, 1994.

Allison Stark Draper, *Boston Massacre: Five Colonists Killed by British Soldiers*. New York: Powerkids, 2003.

Laurie O'Neill, *The Boston Tea Party*. Brookfield, CT: Millbrook, 1996.

Web Sites

The History Place: The American Revolution
www.historyplace.com
One of the many topics covered by The History Place Web site, this series of pages on the Revolution presents time lines of the era. On each time line page, visitors can access information that relates to the period between early colonization and 1790.

Kid Info: American Revolution
www.kidinfo.com
This Web site gathers links to other sites devoted to some aspect of the Revolution. This is a good place to track down further information on a specific topic of interest.

Liberty: The American Revolution
www.pbs.org
A companion to the PBS documentary miniseries on the Revolution, this Web site is an excellent resource for students.

INDEX